PIXEL ART
Coloring book for kids

Children's Coloring Books, Kids Activities

16 Different figures to draw & Color

This book belongs to:

_____

_____

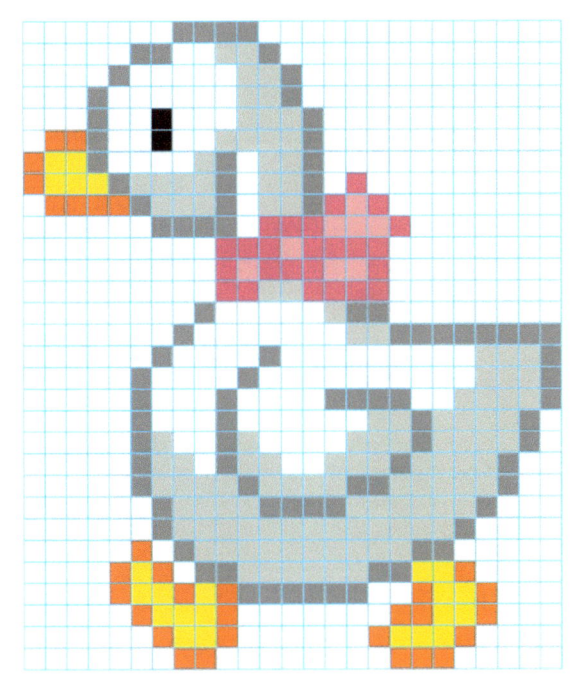

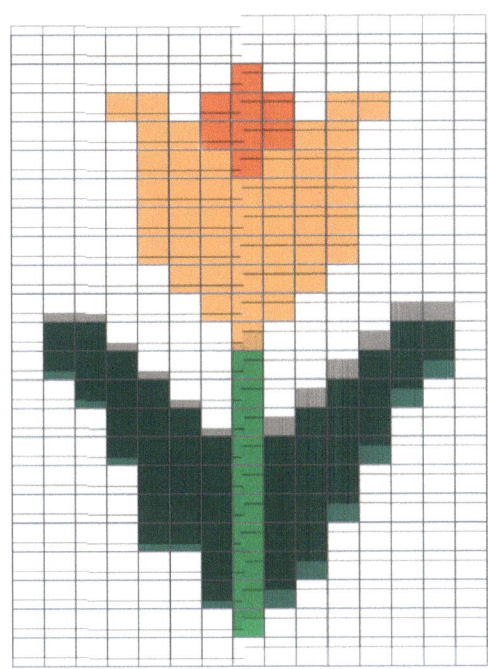

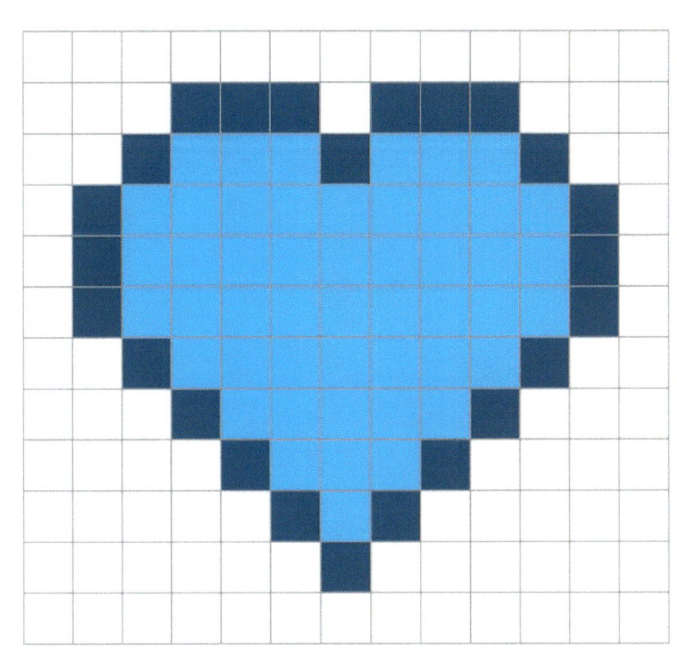

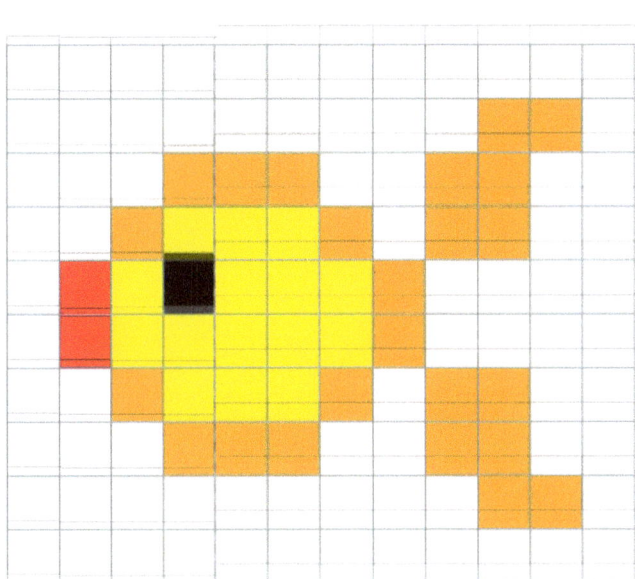

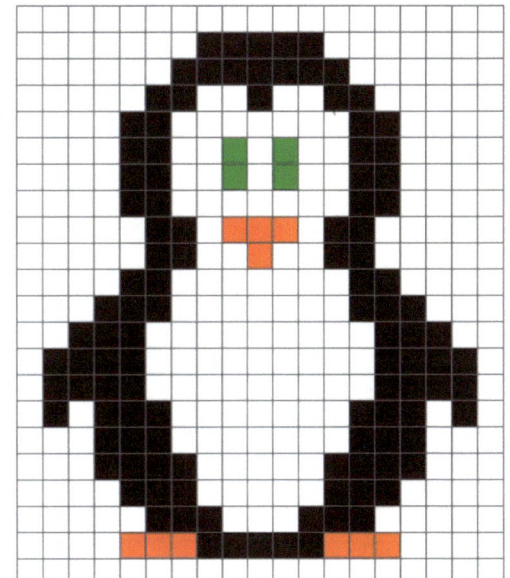

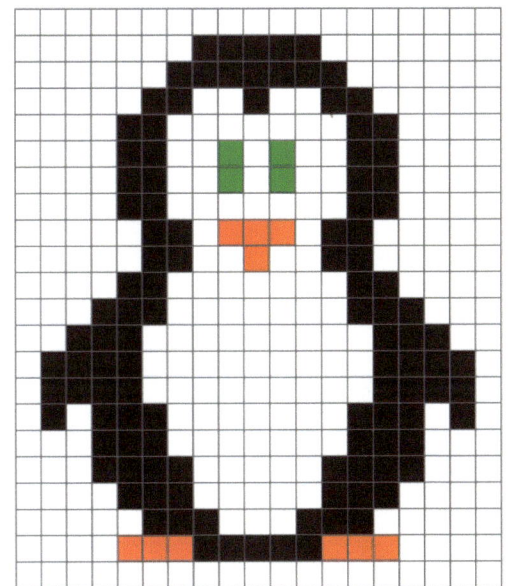

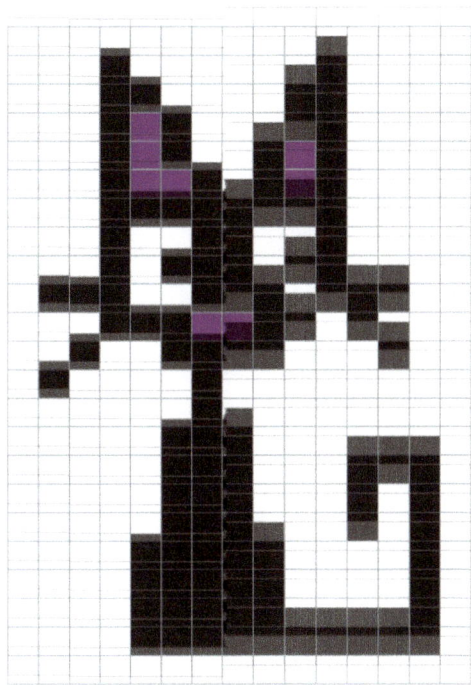

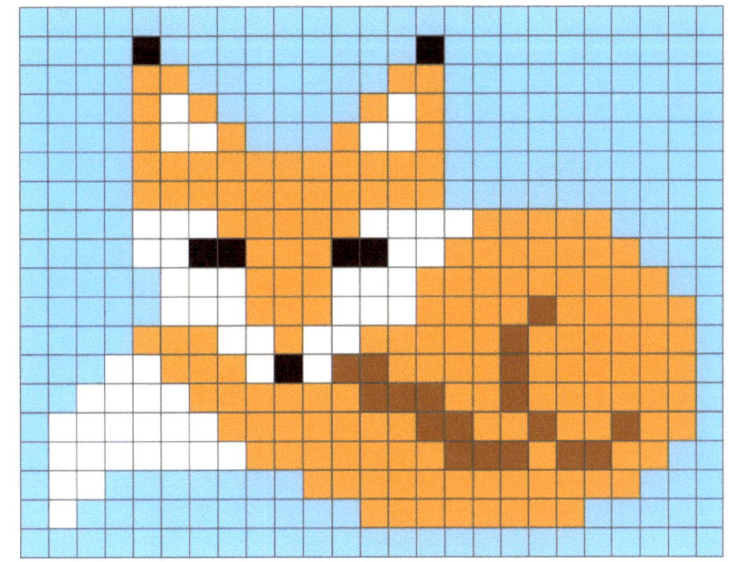

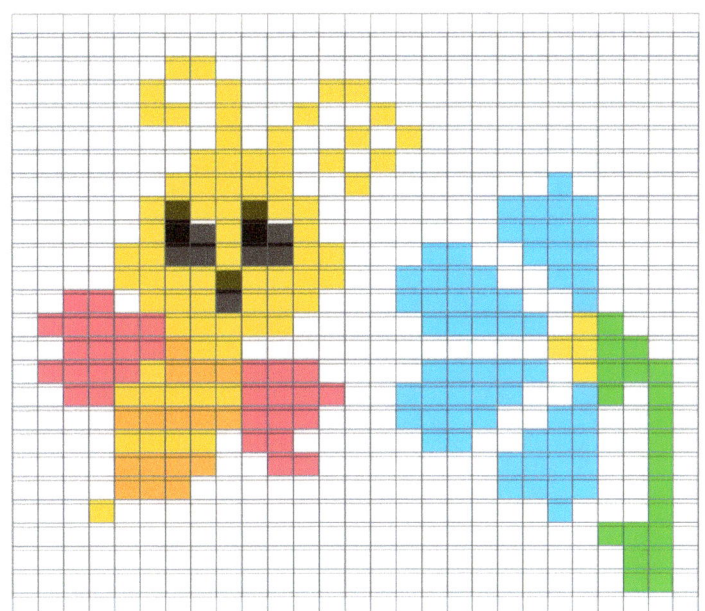

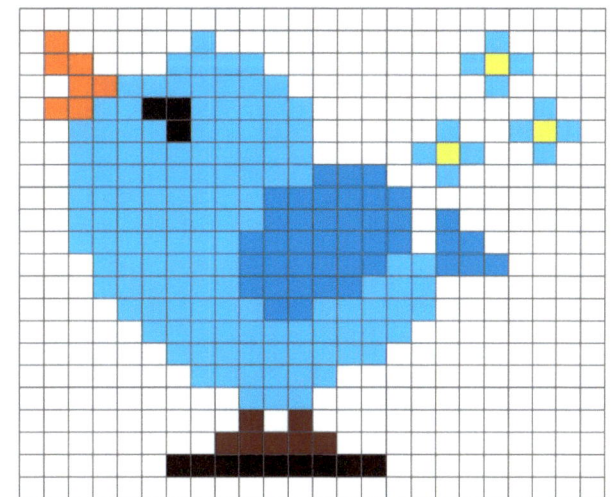

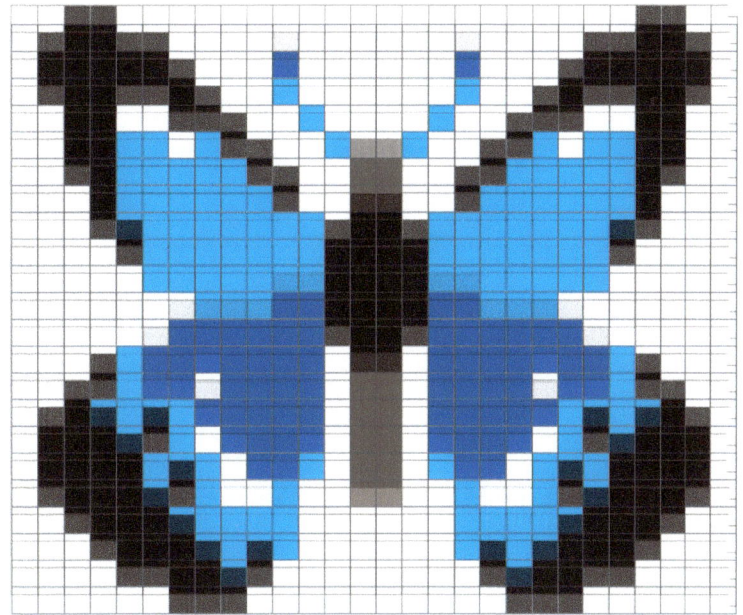

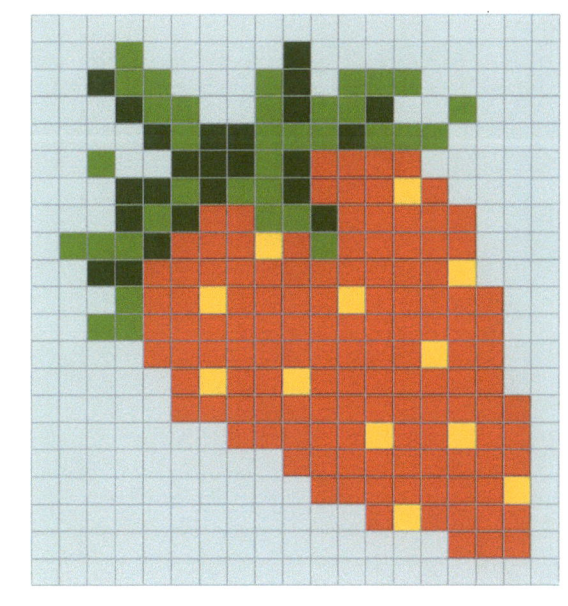

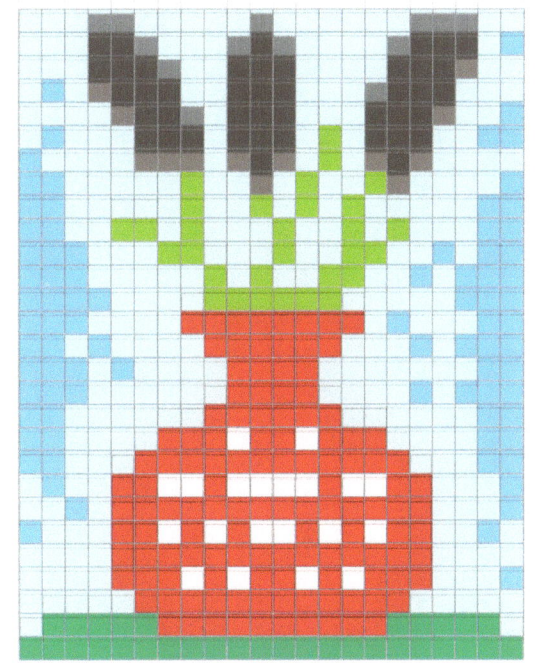

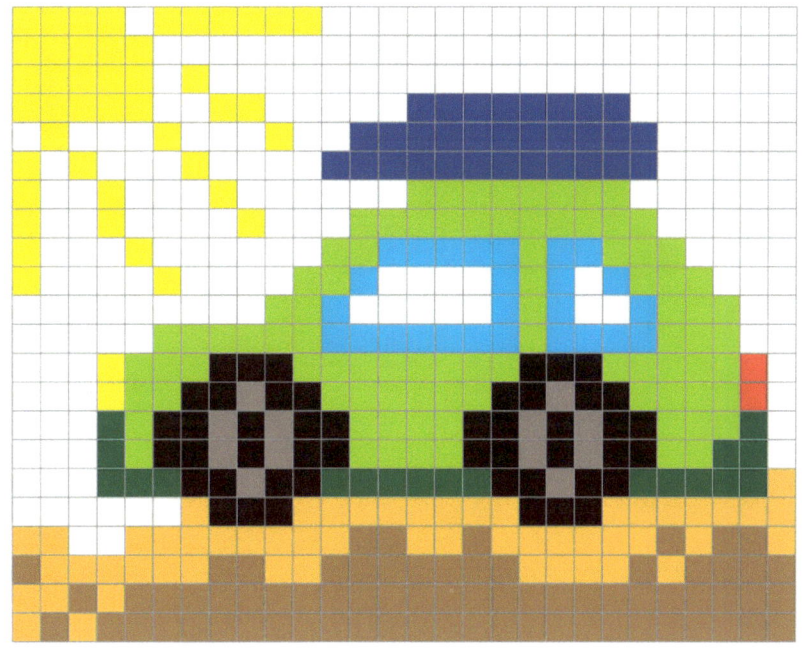

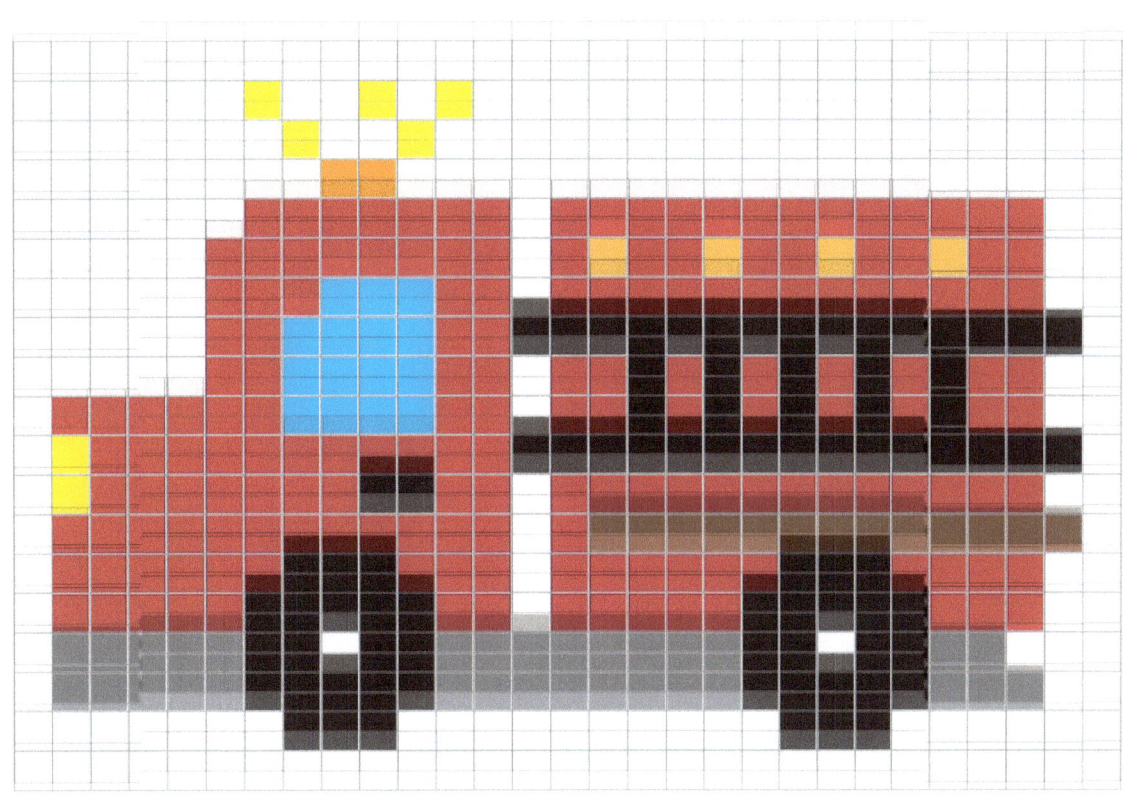

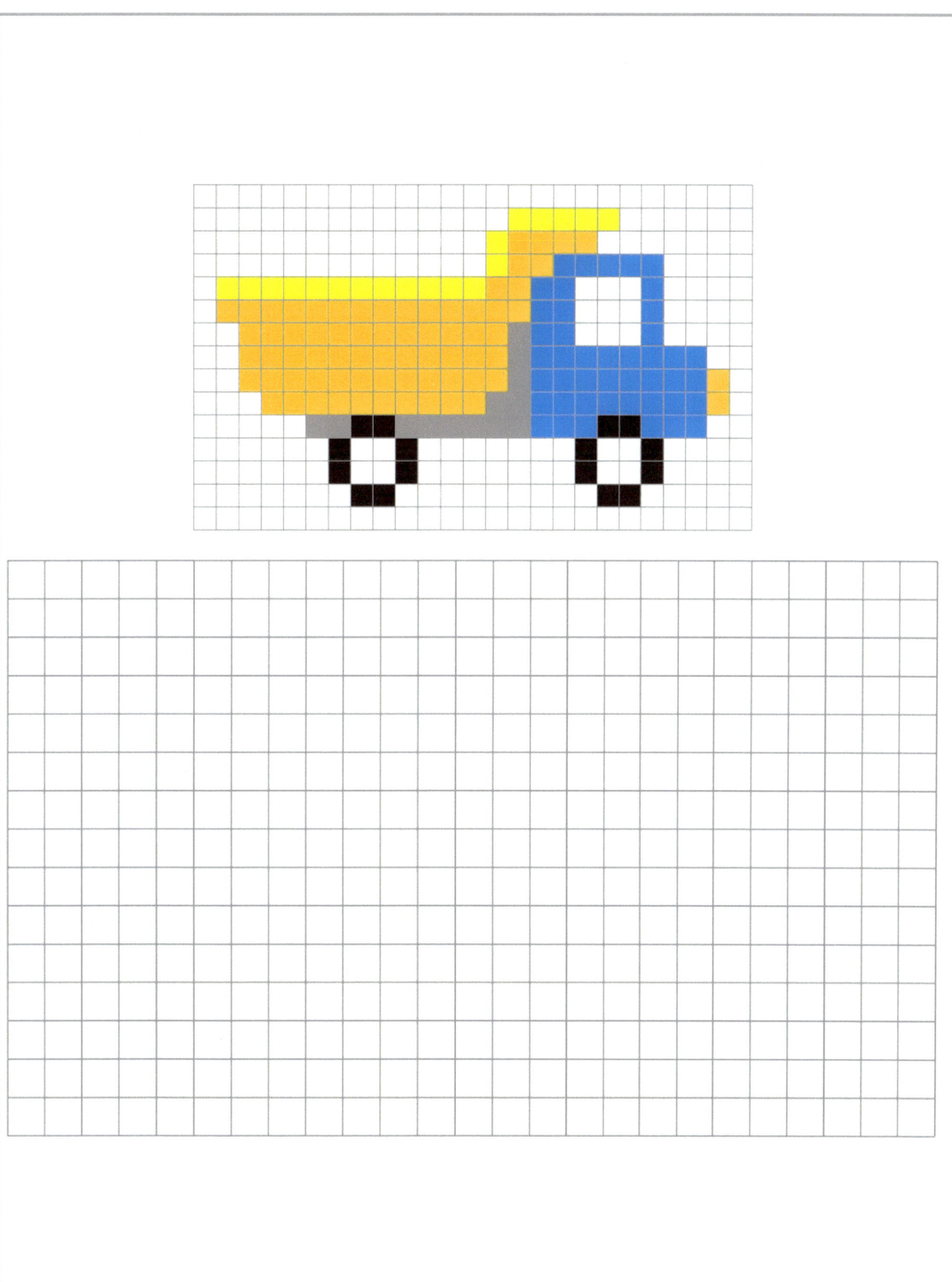

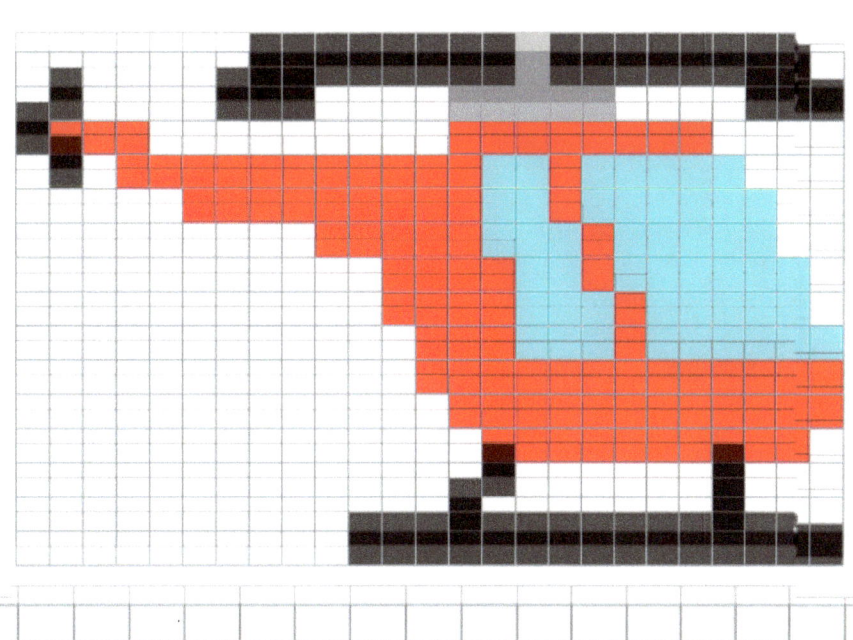

www.ingramcontent.com/pod-product-compliance
Lightning Source LLC
Chambersburg PA
CBHW051938210526
45473CB00006B/2292